Light As A Feather
42 Laws of Maat for children

by Kajara Nia Yaa Nebthet
Art by ADOFO

published by Ra Sekhi Arts Temple Sept 2015

Light As a Feather

The 42 Laws of MAAT for Children

This book is dedicated to the Goddess MAAT.

© Copyright 2016 by Ra Sekhi Arts Temple

All Rights Reserved. No part of this book may be reproduced or utilized in any form or by any means, electronic or mechanical, including photocopying, recording, or by any information storage and retrieval system, without written permission from the publisher. Published in the United States.

When we do our best

To honor these laws,

We keep our hearts

As light as a Feather.

A long, long time ago,
People lived in peace and harmony.

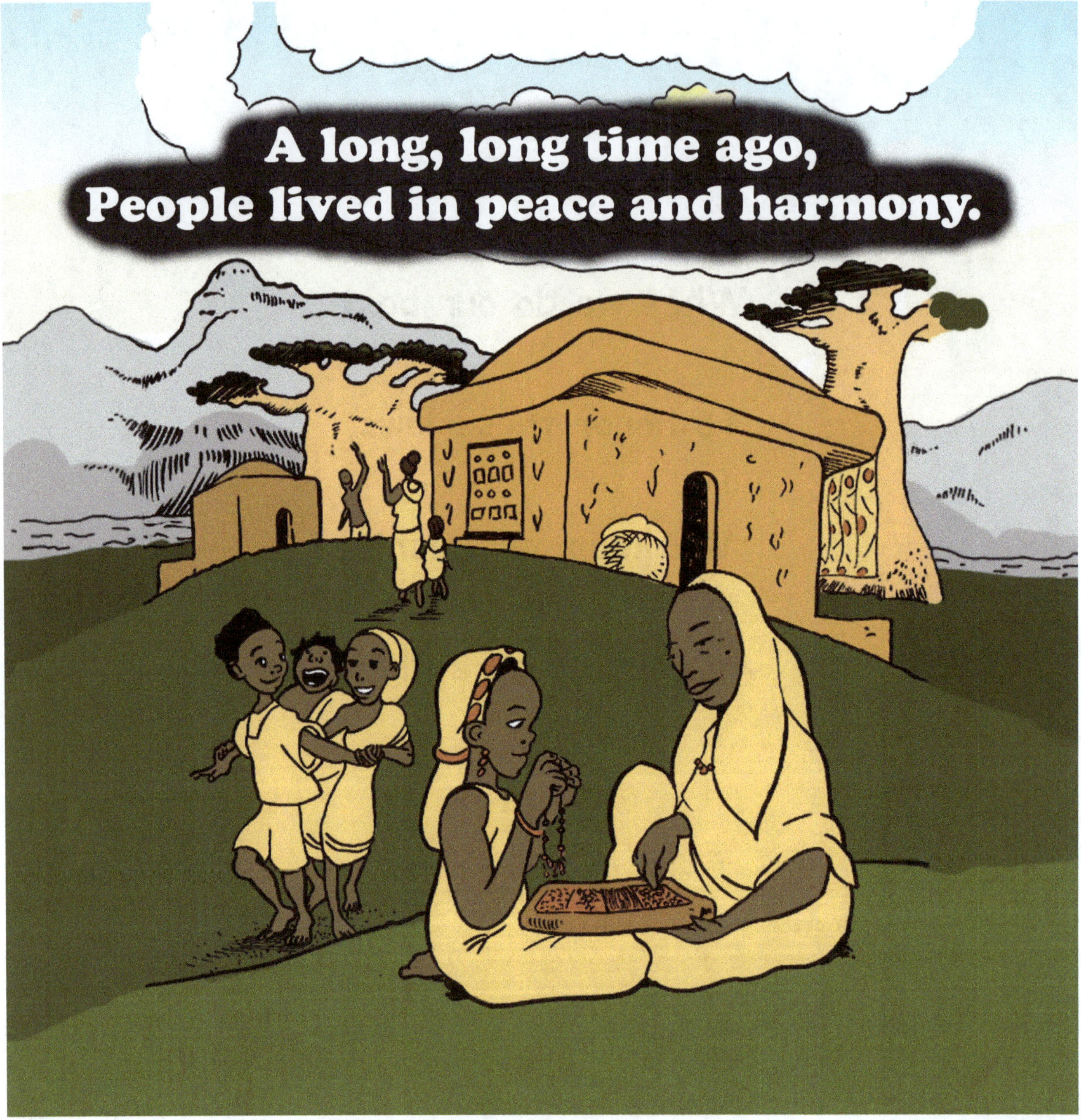

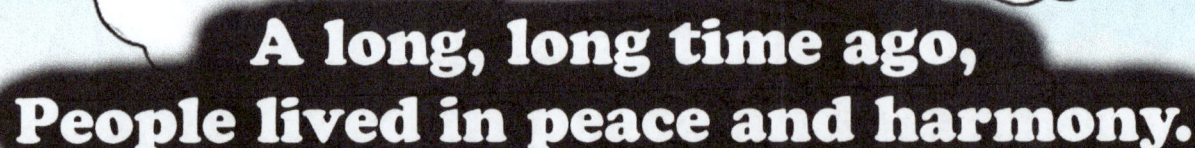

MAAT is a Goddess from Ancient Kemet.

She represents truth, order and justice.

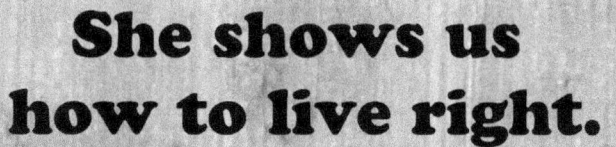

She shows us how to live right.

These are her laws.

MAAT is known as an aspect of NTR, which is an ancient name of THE CREATOR (GOD). She represents order, balance, harmony, justice, truth, reciprocity and compassion. She is seen with wings and a feather on her crown. She is one of the most ancient deities of Ancient Kemet, also known as Egypt. She has been loved and honored by many for thousands of years.

The laws of MAAT were written on the walls of the pyramids thousands of years ago. They were left there to remind us of how we are supposed to live and behave. When we live with these principles we are living with MAAT.

Our Ancient Kemetic Ancestors lived with high morals, high standards, and high intelligence. This is our legacy and our birthright. This is also the key to our healing and becoming great people once again.

There are many translations of the laws of MAAT. This version was translated especially for children. They can be recited daily and memorized. They can also be helpful to recite when little ones need a reminder of good behavior.

42 LAWS OF MAAT

1. I WILL NOT DO WRONG
2. I WILL NOT STEAL
3. I WILL NOT ACT WITH VIOLENCE
4. I WILL NOT KILL
5. I WILL NOT BE UNJUST
6. I WILL NOT CAUSE PAIN
7. I WILL NOT WASTE FOOD
8. I WILL NOT LIE
9. I WILL NOT DESECRATE HOLY PLACES
10. I WILL NOT SPEAK EVIL
11. I WILL NOT ABUSE MY SEXUALITY
12. I WILL NOT CAUSE THE SHEDDING OF TEARS
13. I WILL NOT SOW SEEDS OF REGRET
14. I WILL NOT BE AN AGGRESSOR
15. I WILL NOT ACT GUILEFUL
16. I WILL NOT LAY WASTE THE PLOWED LAND
17. I WILL NOT BEAR FALSE WITNESS
18. I WILL NOT SPEAK AGAINST ANY PERSON
19. I WILL NOT BE WRATHFUL & ANGRY
20. I WILL NOT LAY WITH A MAN'S WIFE
21. I WILL NOT LAY WITH A WOMAN'S HUSBAND

22 I WILL NOT POLLUTE MYSELF
23 I WILL NOT CAUSE TERROR
24 I WILL NOT POLLUTE THE EARTH
25 I WILL NOT SPEAK IN ANGER
26 I WILL NOT TURN FROM WORDS OF TRUTH
27 I WILL NOT UTTER CURSES
28 I WILL NOT INITIATE A QUARREL
29 I WILL NOT BE EXCITABLE OR CONTENTIOUS
30 I WILL NOT BE PREJUDICE
31 I WILL NOT BE AN EAVESDROPPER
32 I WILL NOT SPEAK OVERMUCH
33 I WILL NOT ACT AGAINST MY ANCESTORS
34 I WILL NOT WASTE WATER
35 I WILL NOT DO EVIL
36 I WILL NOT BE ARROGANT
37 I WILL NOT BLASPHEME THE ONE MOST HIGH
38 I WILL NOT COMMIT FRAUD
39 I WILL NOT DEFRAUD TEMPLE OFFERINGS
40 I WILL NOT PLUNDER THE DEAD
41 I WILL NOT MISTREAT CHILDREN
42 I WILL NOT MISTREAT ANIMALS

Translated by Heru Semahj of The Shrine of Ptah

Rekhit Kajara Nia Yaa Nebthet is an author, healer, priestess, teacher, artist and founder of the Ra Sekhi Arts Temple. She has dedicated her life to heal and teach people to be more healthy and to take better care of themselves. She has been a teacher for over 20 years. This is her second children's book.
Email Rekhit Kajara at rasekhitemple@gmail.com
Visit www.rasekhihealing.com
 and www.rasekhistore.com

Elihu ADOFO Bey is a full-time freelance illustrator who grew up in East Orange NJ, moved to Atlanta Ga. and presently works out of Goldsboro NC and Jamaica NY.

Visit: www.adofoillustrations.bigcartel.com
facebook: Art by Adofo
Email: adofoillustrations@gmail.com

www.ingramcontent.com/pod-product-compliance
Lightning Source LLC
Chambersburg PA
CBHW060428010526
44118CB00017B/2405